LIVES
AND
TIMES

Mohandas Gandhi

John Barraclough

Heinemann Interactive Library,
Des Plaines, Illinois

Published by Heinemann Interactive Library,
an imprint of Reed Educational & Professional Publishing,
1350 East Touhy Avenue, Suite 240 West
Des Plaines, IL 60018

Printed in Hong Kong / China
Designed by Ken Vail Graphic Design.
Illustrations by Shirley Tourett

02 01 00 99
10 9 8 7 6 5 4 3 2

Library of Congress Cataloging-in-Publication Data

Barraclough, John, 1960-
    Mohandas Gandhi/John Barraclough,
        p. cm. -- (lives and times)
    Includes bibliographical references and index.
    ISBN 1-57572-561-4 (lib. bdg.)
        1. Ghandi , Mahatma, 1869–1948 -- Juvenile literature. 2. Statesmen -- India --
Biography -- Juvenile literature. 3. Nationalists -- India -- Biography -- Juvenile
literature. I. Title. II. Series: Lives and times (Crystal Lake, Ill.)
DS481.G3B355 1997
954.03'5'092 -- dc21
(B)   97-19301
                                                                          CIP
                                                                           AC

Some words are shown in bold, **like this**.
You can find out what they mean by looking
in the glossary. The glossary also helps you say
difficult words.

Acknowledgments
The author and publishers are grateful to the following for permission to reproduce copyright photographs:
The New York Times, p. 22;
Topham Picturepoint, pp.18, 19, 20, 21.

Cover photograph: Hulton Getty

Special thanks to Betty Root for her comments in the preparation of this book.

Contents

Part One

Mohandas Gandhi was born in India in 1869, about 130 years ago. When he was a little boy, he was afraid of the dark. He always slept with a night-light.

Gandhi and his family were **Hindu**.
When he was thirteen he had an
arranged marriage. His parents chose his
wife. He and his wife, **Kasturbai**, did not
live together until they were adults.

In 1888, when he was nineteen, Gandhi
went to London, England, to learn
how to be a **lawyer**. He was lonely
and homesick for India. He missed
his wife **Kasturbai**.

In 1893, Gandhi went to work in
South Africa. One day, he was thrown
off a train because another passenger
didn't like Indians.

This **racism** made Gandhi angry.
He began to fight racism, but peacefully.
One day, he stopped police horses
charging at a crowd by making everyone
lie on the ground. He knew that the horses
would not want to step on people.

In 1915, Gandhi went back to India. Many
people had heard of his work against racism.
When the ship he was on landed Gandhi
was treated like a hero. He was nicknamed
"**Mahatma.**" This means "Great Soul."

Britain **ruled** India at this time. Many Indians did not like this. In 1919, British soldiers shot at a crowd of 400 peaceful **protestors.** Gandhi believed that British rule had to end.

Gandhi became a great leader of the Indian people. He held many peaceful meetings to show the British that they should leave India and stop ruling there.

In 1931 Gandhi went to London to talk to the British **Prime Minister**. He agreed with many of Gandhi's ideas, but he still said that the British would not leave India.

After he returned to India, Gandhi was arrested for trying to change things. During his life, he spent a total of seven years in prison. He spent much of his time thinking and spinning cotton.

On August 15, 1947, the British left India. India became **independent**. The Indian flag could at last be flown. This huge country was then split into two countries, India and Pakistan.

Many people all over the world loved
Gandhi and had agreed with his ideas
about making India independent. Yet on
January 30, 1948, a gunman killed him
as he went to pray.

Gandhi's last words were "Hay Rama." This means "Oh God." The **Prime Minister** of India said, "The light has gone out of our lives."

One million people went to Gandhi's funeral. He was India's greatest leader. Gandhi's ideas and ways of doing things are still admired and followed today.

Part Two

This photograph shows Gandhi when he was seven. He was a shy boy. His mother was very religious. She taught Gandhi to always be truthful and to think of others.

Gandhi was a **vegetarian**. This photograph shows him in London in 1890. He is with members of a vegetarian club where he made friends. He is in the bottom row, on the right.

In London and South Africa, Gandhi wore very nice clothes. When he was 44 years old he decided to dress simply, like the common people of India.

Gandhi was very popular with everyone.
This photograph shows him in England
in 1931, laughing and joking with
factory workers.

This newspaper article from *The New York Times* is about Gandhi's **fasting**. It describes how Gandhi was ready to starve himself to death to get unfair laws changed.

The New York Times.

d as Second-Class Matter, office, New York, N. Y.

NEW YORK, WEDNESDAY, SEPTEMBER 21, 1932 ★★★★ + TW

M'KEE SAYS BANKERS FORCE BUDGET CUTS; DR. NORRIS RESIGNS

Loans to Stop if $80,000,000 Is Not Slashed, Aid Pledged for Public Works if It Is.

MAYOR ACCEPTS ULTIMATUM

"Determined" to Get Economy, He Repeats—Office Working Nights to Rush Schedules.

NORRIS QUITS IN PROTEST

Medical Examiner Resents 20% Cut for Bureau—City Gets Offer for Model Housing Development.

Forging ahead yesterday toward budget economy as a means of ob-

CURRY AND M'COOEY

Gandhi, Tired and Ill, Begins His Death Fast After Hearty Meal and Prayer for Strength

Wireless to THE NEW YORK TIMES.

BOMBAY, Sept. 20. — Mahatma Gandhi solemnly began his "fast unto death" today behind the walls of Yerovda jail at Poona.

Exhausted by the strain of the past few days, the 63-year-old Mahatma was ill and under a doctor's care as he started his fateful hunger strike. He has had heavy correspondence and a colossal number of telegrams to deal with ever since he announced he would starve to death as a protest against the government's communal settlement. In view of his condition, the prison physician decided not to allow visitors to see him this morning.

All over India Hindus ceased work. Thousands went to the temples to pray for the Mahatma. Other thousands shuttered their shops or stayed away from their work at the factories as a gesture of sorrow.

Mr. Gandhi had a substantial meal before beginning his long, slow ordeal. He had his usual dates, soaked in water, and with them he ate whole-meal bread, tomatoes, oranges and curd. Then, visibly agitated, his secretary, Mahadev Desai, handed him a glass of lemon juice and soda.

This was the last sustenance he will touch, except for water.

When his last meal was finished, the Mahatma quietly announced his fast had started, and knelt to pray, with Vallabhai Patel, the All-India Nationalist Congress leader, and Mr. Desai kneeling alongside him.

A strangely subdued tension gripped the big Hindu centres of India as his fast began. Bombay's Hindu business quarters were deserted. The cotton and bullion markets and the Stock Exchange were closed. Nineteen cotton mills had to suspend because their workers failed to appear. Many schools and colleges were forced to shut their doors because so few students reported for classes. In the European and Moslem quarters, however, business went on as usual without interference.

The most significant event of the day was the admission of the "untouchables" for the first time to certain Hindu temples in Bombay, Nasik and Ahmedabad.

Despite the opposition of the ortho-

Continued on Page Eight.

FINDS RACKETS COST

LA FOLLETTE BEATEN IN WISCONSIN FIGHT; DR. LOVE LOSES HERE

Kohler, Conservative, Named for Governor—Youngman Leads in Bay State.

MRS. PRATT WINS IN CITY

McCooey Man Defeats Dr. Love in State Senate Race—Hastings Renominated.

MIX-UP OVER BALLOTS HERE

Patrolman and Boy Are Shot in Dispute at Polls—Roosevelt Scores Victory Up-State.

Voters in New York, Massachusetts and Wisconsin went to the polls yesterday for the last of the State

22

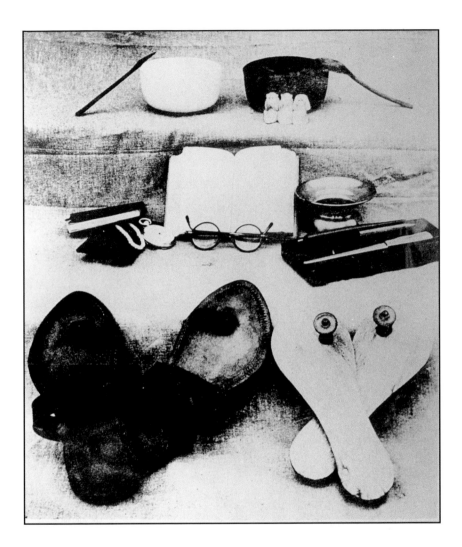

Gandhi believed in living simply. This picture shows the only things he owned when he died. Together, they were only worth about $4.00.

Glossary

This glossary explains difficult words, and helps you to say words which may be hard to say.

fasting Not eating anything.

Hindu Many Indians follow the Hindu religion, which is one of the main world religions. Hindus believe that if you lead a good life, you will be reborn as a better person. You say *HIHN doo.*

independent Free from control by others.

Kasturbai You say *KAST ur by.*

lawyer Person who has studied law, and knows all the rules that people should follow in a country.

Prime Minister Name of the head of the government in some countries.

protester Someone who shows in public that they disagree with something.

Mahatma You say *muh HAHT ma.*

Mohandas You say *moh HAHN das.*

racism Hating somebody just because they are from a different country or have a different color of skin.

rule Be in control.

vegetarian Someone who doesn't eat meat or fish.

Index

More Books to Read

Nicholoson, Michael. *Mahatma Gandhi: Champion of Human Rights.* Milwaukee: Gareth Stevens, 1990.

6725

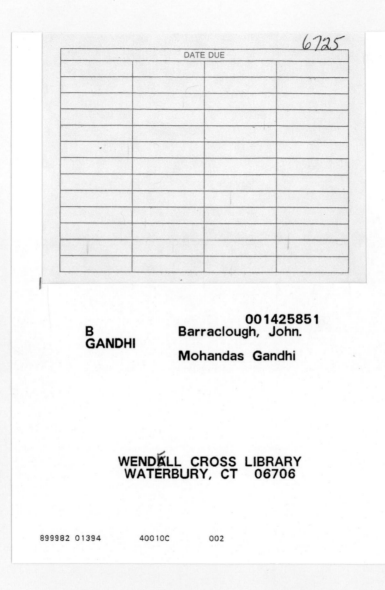

DATE DUE			

**B
GANDHI**

001425851
Barraclough, John.

Mohandas Gandhi